In Love, in Friendship

Henry Johnson

In Love, in Friendship

Vanguard Press

VANGUARD PAPERBACK

© Copyright 2024
Henry Johnson

The right of Henry Johnson to be identified as author of this work has been asserted by him in accordance with the Copyright, Designs and Patents Act 1988.

All Rights Reserved

No reproduction, copy or transmission of this publication may be made without written permission.
No paragraph of this publication may be reproduced, copied or transmitted save with the written permission of the publisher, or in accordance with the provisions of the Copyright Act 1956 (as amended).

Any person who commits any unauthorised act in relation to this publication may be liable to criminal prosecution and civil claims for damages.

A CIP catalogue record for this title is available from the British Library.

ISBN 978 1 80016 786 5

This is a work of fiction. Names, characters, businesses, places, events and incidents are either the product of the author's imagination or used in a fictitious manner. Any resemblance to actual persons, living or dead, or actual events is purely coincidental.

*Vanguard Press is an imprint of
Pegasus Elliot Mackenzie Publishers Ltd.*
www.pegasuspublishers.com

First Published in 2024

**Vanguard Press
Sheraton House Castle Park
Cambridge England**

Printed & Bound in Great Britain

Countdown to Now and Forever

Years have passed since I held you in my arms,
Months to go until you and I share the same ground.
Minutes since we last spoke.
Time, when focused on, feels like a mean-spirited joke.

But to me, there is no distance in time,
With my love, a comfort I find.
Not a second has passed without you,
In my heart and soul, no need is due.

Since we first met, time has been on our side,
Each moment we share, I have enjoyed the ride.
A grain of sand stands in mid-air,
Time may pass as if it was never there.

We share a life with you there,
Yet my need for you brings no fear.
I am yours, however, you will have me,
Now and forever, time has no meaning.

Henry

Accidentally Romantic

Was it an accident when I matched?
With my best friend on OkCupid?
Now we are so close nothing comes between us
But with all the signs I have to ask if we are being stupid.
Bookstores, texting, hour-long phone calls,
                and going to dinner after running together
   in the rain
I wouldn't risk anything to change a second together,
But I do wonder if our friendship is something too tame.
Over 900 miles between our lips,
And 1,357 days between our only date,
Am I insane to question?
Or is more than friendship our fate?
Am I a fool?
Are you the wise one?
For considering the signs,
Or letting things rest as just fun?
So many bumpy long roads between us,
So many challenges ahead,
Is it even worth the question,
If those are the real signs which should be read?
More than infatuation,
But definitely not just lust
Are the signs screaming we belong together?
Or, am I just an old man in a rush?
I love you in a way
I have tried to define,

But anyway you are in my life
That dynamic to me is fine.
I love you more than touch
I love you more than need,
If the universe guides us to more than friendship
The signs are not up to me alone to read.

        Henry

Sometimes

Sometimes when I miss your call,
    I am just as happy knowing you want to chat with me,
    Sometimes I think whatever else I was doing,
    Was the least important thing in the world.

    Sometimes when I am talking with you,
    I know that I am right where I am supposed to be,
    Sometimes I wonder how I can feel,
    Like a person thousands of miles away could feel like home.

    Sometimes I know you,
    Then others I fear that this is all it will ever be
    Sometimes I am the unfair one
    Other times I question why you can be here

    Sometimes I see a chance
    Others I see the worst consequences
    Sometimes nothing else matters but you
    Then I remember love is a two-way street.

    Sometimes I want to destroy a world,

A world without you by my side
Sometimes I feel guilty
Because what we have is still so beautiful.

Sometimes I want you to be mine
Others, I realize you are all I need
Sometimes I want to hold you
Others, I fear clipping your wings

Sometimes I only love you,
Others, I love what you have helped me become,
Sometimes I get greedy and want more,
I always will be here for you.

Henry

To a Beautiful Black Woman

I have accepted in my mind that my heart will never fully know you
    It is yours to the capacity of what shade it is capable,
    Everything else inside of me screams I know you.
    I would love to look upon you as much is allowable
    Your laugh is honey to my ears
    Your face, your skin, your brilliant mind,
    Everything that you are mirrors,
    The very definition of beauty I am able to find
    I want to be the one who wipes away your tears
    And holds you in tender moments shared
    I have known you in all ways but touch,
    But that is a lie, for while I feel anger, you the pain of fear,
    I want to splinter myself into a billion pieces
    And watch over you by improving the species
    But the most justice I am capable of doing,
    Is accept your life experiences and listen and silence my rudeness
    You never should be made to feel,

Injustice with origins outside my empathetic grasp.
But even if I was your personal knight errant,
Needing my services gives others' responsibilities a pass
I will always be here to give you my all,
I can listen, hold you, or try if you call,
You are the most beautiful woman I have ever met
Anyone who doesn't treat you and everyone else here on earth with justice deserves no respect.
I would trudge through any soil,
Just to be worthy of holding your hand
While I hope for more,
I wait for a yes.

Henry

This Invisible Wall

Between us,
    Not the miles.
    I hear you,
    But the unsaid causes a gasp.

    Coyness,
    Makes me want you more,
    I want every bit of you,
    Till my breath's last

    Your silence
    Will come down
    Brick by brick
    I see with blind eyes into your heart.

    Not yet spoken,
    But present
    And felt
    You seem unknowing, but I am smart

    You are glowing
    As only one who appears
    To reciprocate my love,
    We are walking a path together

    Our hearts
    Know this is right

This is real,
    We cannot deceive each other's

I have set
 My sights on you
Hold out as long as you can.
But you know our love for each other is
true.

Henry

My Birthday Queen

There is a birthday queen,
        I may be over two years her senior,
        But she strips off my years,
        Leaving my decades of baggage pounds
leaner.

        Her presence clears me
        Of all fear, doubt, and pain,
        Her love
        Has my heart's service behind her reign

        A man of years
        Past reckless foolishness of youth
        Caution in my birthday queen's service
        Is unattainable, as my self-preservation is
aloof.

        I would feel even the fiercest beasts
        Just to present her with a trophy
        No monster, ghost, or demon
        Shall escape me.

        Thirty-eight, my birthday queen,
        Brings youth to a heart in love,
        Years to pass,
        For me, her heart, to budge.

I wish the world for you,
And you to feel the youth you give me
Our friendship
Is the greatest gift from my birthday queen.

Henry

A Familiar Feeling

There they are,
>I want to love them,
>Like coffee once was
>But still not loved
>I love everything about
>The idea of them
>Should I love them more?

>I still give them a chance
>Hoping I have changed
>And this thing which I think
>Will make me happy
>Might bring me the feeling I
>Want so badly
>But they are not my favorite

>In my mind, they have a taste
>Better than any other sandwich
>I will ever have
>But when I taste one
>The love is not there in the moment
>So why do I keep having them?
>What is wrong with me?

>Do I settle for disappointment?
>With every deception, I tell myself?
>One day will they taste like I want them to

Will my feelings magically change?
Can I be loved?
And earn that love?
Or will I always be your pierogi sandwich?

I will stay on the menu if you ever want to try one more time.
There are worse fates than being your pierogi sandwich.
I am the best pierogi sandwich I can be,
Maybe someday you will change your taste,
And I will be exactly what you want,
But I learned a long time ago:
You are what you love,
Not what loves you.
Thank you for helping me become,
One of the greatest pierogi sandwiches of all time.
I will always love you for what I have become
By being on your menu.

Henry

You Returned My Call

After our one date, I wasn't sure
                You were my first, that I saw going the distance
                But I had been wrong before, I needed a sign
                I needed to see if you were the one or if there was romantic resistance
                I had an amazing date, I stole a kiss
                Fearing I gave away too much too soon
                I apologized even though I stole it out of need.
                I backed off and waited, if this was the real thing, I would give you room.
                I reached out a week or so later, I feared I was wrong, but I called
                You didn't answer, and I thought my gauge was broken
                Then you returned my call, and I set a goal of being worthy of you
                Since that day I have put in all the work to earn the words I needed spoken
                You were the one, but life is cruel and unfair
                I would and will fight to earn you, knowing it would be hard
                You and I ending up together, no matter how bad I want it is not guaranteed

The realization that I wanted you in a way that might not be in the cards

Thirty-nineth birthday I planned to ask you to be mine

Then I lost my nerve because I knew I wasn't ready

Then claimed by another wonderful person, which ended in a worthy friendship

All while my goal to be with you remained steady.

I said it, I love you, you said it back to me

But only as friends, we headed down parallel but different paths

Now I feel like our paths, even right next to each other are in need of joining

What I wouldn't do to combine romantic love amongst our laughs.

You reached back out to me and gave me hope

So precious, so beautiful, so worth my all

Will you return my love, and be mine?

Like you made yourself my life's goal, when you returned my call.

Henry

To be your Future Trophy

What I am, and how I feel about that
        Is not who I plan to be,
        So much work, but there is time
        Before my pride is reflected in thee

        I want to be a source of pride
        Both my own and yours
        I am guided by my love for you
        To become someone which we both respect more.

        I want to be bragged about
        By you to all of your friends
        I want to feel secure knowing that I'm above all bars
        Not a single one for me bent

        I want to become that trophy
        That you, the person I admire, holds
        I want to be such a prize
        That you see me as the new mold

        I want to be the best
        In the future, I will become
        Someone whose current flaws
        Are distantly joked about for fun

I love myself, as I do you
But still have room to grow
To earn us being in love
To us a trophy I will show.

Henry

Good Girl

You are a good girl
          You like being called that, don't you?
          I have never called a woman good girl
          But I will to you, as you I woo
          I haven't come close
          To earning the right
          To place my hand on your neck
          But for you, if asked I might
          Anything if given the chance
          Anything if I am deemed worthy
          To take you to the place
          Which to discuss now is still too early
          I will write you my feelings
          I will wait my whole life
          But when our time comes, my poetic verses
          will be replaced by the arc of your back
          I will do any and everything you like
          To please you I may only get one chance
          Every position, every move
          I will work your body from the first second to our last
          You have known I think about you
          Or at least my mind is open to you in this way
          But only if you ask me
          Will anything happen in May

I want to please you
I want to be your best
But only if it enhances us
If you do not ask, it will stay at rest.

Henry

Free to Be Free

You are free to be free,
                No one owns you
                        I will never own you
                                Even though I hope to love your body
                        Any dick you choose
                Mine, or not, or other
                        You are free to be free
                Anyone who can please you
                        That you choose to allow that freedom
                Is lucky for the time they share with you
                      My rights are none
                            Except to love
                      And share your body if it is ever offered
                If that day never comes
                      Then I will not be hurt
                          Only lucky to have you so close to me
                      In every other way
                          Any man who gets you to the place
                      I have taken myself so many times
                          While thinking of being free with you

                    Even while so far away
                    Is no more inspiring of jealousy
                        Then one of your toys
                    I have the greatest gift
                        That   no   one   has
challenged me yet for
                    I have the freedom to keep you
free
                        And if you ever choose to
let me share your body
                        There will be not even the goldest
of chains
                        You are and will always be
            free to be free
            I would have it no other way.

            Henry

With Me or Not with Me

Whether you are mine or another's
        Freely fucking or sharing secrets,
        I will always love you

        Whether we text every day
        Or hold each other as we fall asleep
        Every day with you in my life is a new high

        Whether naughty or nice
        At each other's place or separate
        I wear you on my heart

        Whether alone or with another
        You are still my favorite person
        To share in life's best moments with.

        With me or not with me
        You are my eternal fountain
        Of deep gratitude for being alive.

        Whether naked or clothed
        Inside of you or 900 miles away
        You have helped me love myself

        Whether happy or sad
        I know you are there

And neither of us are alone

Whether here or there
I do not care
As long as I do right by you.

Henry

Your Last Dick(s)

Someday,
    Hopefully way off in the future,
    You will have your last dick(s),
    Someday,
    Will be the last time
    You feel a dick inside you
    Someday,
    Even in you have,
    A dick in your mouth and
    One in your pussy,
    And one in each hand
    And you make them all come at once
    You will have your last dick.
    Someday,
    You will have the choice to have my dick
    Or any other man's you choose
    That also wisely chooses you.
    But humans are mortal,
    So, one day,
    You will have your last dick(s)
    Someday,
    You will look back on your life,
    I hope without a single dick-related regret.
    But before your last dick,
    If you want a dick
    Or dicks,

Live your life free.
Live your life
So that when your last dick comes
You can rest knowing
You got yours.

Henry

Unspoken Secrets (A Secret Poem by Henry Johnson)

I have and will share everything with you
        Except for one thing
        It is not something I will ever be able to share,
        And will bury it so deep in this book,
        That if you ever find it,
        You love my poetry enough
        To discover my unshared poem
        I have a secret
        I will never share
        Unless you find it
        I want to fuck you in the ass.
        I want to pound your asshole
        With my big thick cock
        I want to drain my balls in your asshole
        I want you to love me so much
        That you like my dick in your ass
        And are excited for me to stretch your asshole
        Just because it will get me off harder
        I have never shared this and never will ask
        But if you took this book as more than symbolic
        And took the time to read it
        Know I have jerked off dozens of times
        To the thought

Of me blowing my load in your sweet asshole

Now you know

Thank you for taking the time to read this whole book.

I love you no matter what, and always will.

Henry

You are my Christmas Angel

Nothing could stop me
          From sharing myself in writing
          Then I fell in love with you
          And the terror of what you would think was biting

          Schizoaffective, crazy, hypergraphia
          Words uttered that doesn't define me
          But if you knew how much I loved you
          These words pale in comparison to the misery your judgment would bring.

          When all hope is lost, in the world of mortals
          I find some in a story about the seraph of truth
          He worships the mighty and beautiful seraph of peace
          I stop sharing when She became you.

          While you don't have wings
          Or a sword of light
          You fill me with peace
          And because of you, through the fears I fight

          You are the most beautiful woman

shove

        I have ever loved
        Just telling you how beautiful you are
        Gives me the strength to my deepest fears,

        You are all I want, being in your light
        Is everything to me
        But then those textbook words
        And in reality, I find fear.

us

to me

        I would stand at your side,
        At peace, just knowing you thought true of
        But to share you are more than a goddess
        Rationally I fear will break your trust

        I would walk 900 miles
        Battling any beast of evil
        But your rejection of me, as mad
        Makes my expectations settle.

        I am sorry that I love you this much
        You are more than Freya, or Hera, or Sif
        To me, you are why my heart beats,
        Telling you now, you give me peace.

        I love you,
        As only a better man could

If I have to become the seraph of truth
Then for you my seraph of peace, I would.

You are just Danielle,
And I, just Henry,
But one day, not too far in the distance
I hope, for my love, for you, to be seen.

I cannot think of a better place
to keep my heart safe, than in your light,
and in love with you,
and in your service, it stays bright.

Henry

A Poem Without Words

While I haven't heard your voice today,
        You are still with me in my heart
        Not a single text, Yet even without a spark
        The fire that burns inside needed not this
to start.

        I think about you
        Even with you so far away
        Knowing you exist
        Makes any loneliness stray

        You are my beacon
        Even on days such as this
        Without a single word shared
        Your presence on this planet leaves me
rich

        I love you every morning
        I love you every night
        Even when you are just a thought to me
        My whole world is right

        I love you without a touch
        I may not be able to caress or hold
        But you are my sunshine
        To you my darkness folds

I love you even if you will never have the words

To say the same to me
For I am lucky that I am that which I love
Not what shares it with me.

Henry

It Breaks my Heart

I may never hold you as my own
    I may never see the look in your eyes
    That only a woman in love bears
    But I still hope for it, the greatest surprise.

    I may never sleep naked
    Next to you
    Holding on to my greatest love
    And never being afraid of you to lose

    I may never get a 'yes'
    To a question about being mine forever
    I see a world where dreams are fulfilled
    And another where we never bother

    It breaks my heart
    That I must eventually censor myself
    Shut the secret vault
    Place my secret key on a secret shelf

    The day I no longer can
    Share my feelings
    Even unreciprocated
    Is the day the darkness steals me.

    A hundred poems
    With you away

Just for one chance
For more than a hug.

It breaks my heart
That if I don't stop
I fear I may lose you
Even while apart.

I trust you to tell me
To draw the line
Even shattering this dream
For a friend who pines

When the day comes, I can no longer tell you

About my love
My heart will break
But to my shattered heart, I put you above.

Henry

Two Poems in One Day

One in your morning, One in your night,
        Twice in one day, would give most women a fright

        But you are a good girl and can take twice as much

        Filling you up, putting a dream in touch

        With two in one day, will you look me in the eyes,
        Or the other one, which is in for a surprise?

        Two in one day, if you can take the pleasure
        Then past and present, you will be both our treasures.

        Will you moan, will you cry?
        Will you be so happy to experience two guys?

        At this moment, I hope to rock you,
        Earlier, I was so overwhelmed, away me you blew,

        One at each end, of your day,

Filled to the brim, there may be nothing you can say,

Just shut your eyes, angel, let the two have you

Me and myself, to you, let us do.

What you want, and what we can give.
Two times the love, and two times the true,

Feelings of being filled up, and shared front and back,
The only one I am jealous of is the one who makes you lose track,

Of all your worry, all your stress,
Two poems in one day, can make quite an emotional mess.

Henry

The Dream of Coming Together

Will I ever be yours? 900 miles apart seems to suggest no.

Will we ever come together, or is all this affection and attention for show?

I may not be able to build you a house, but when you give me a chance,

I will build a life with you, a life to have and to hold, to be yours till our last naked dance.

I want to be with you, I want to be your man in a way that you never feel unsafe

If building a life means starting my own, to beckon you home, mine becoming our place.

I want you in every way, as husband and wife, deviant sex partners, and lazy bums on the couch

My adventure to capture your heart, and lay with you, and grow old as your childish grouch

Begins when I start a life of my own, away from my family

Even a decade of loneliness, is nothing, if afterward, you spend my life with me.

You are the one, my soul's loving quest

I want to be the man who sleeps head on your breasts

You are my everything, which makes me want more for me

If the most beautiful, kind, and wonderful woman in the world is the icing, I will embrace greed

My God, how I love you and want you,

Just a few big life steps to be worthy of life anew.

I want to keep you warm on cold nights, and make you laugh with my imperfect jokes,

But first I need a place we could start a life together, to test the ropes.

Buy a place, rent a place, as long as it is a home

A place for you to visit me until you no longer wish to roam.

This adventure will not be of the mind, it will be one of growing up

But if it gets me a chance with you, I will move my stuff.

It will not be overnight, or all at once.

But with the right factors, I will have a nice enough place, for your heart to hunt.

All the jokes, all the rhymes, it has come time for me to grow up

But while you say I am plenty manly enough, having somewhere of my own is ideal after I take you out.

You have been generous and given me time,

This is not about poems, or presents, this is about making you mine.

I will become a man worthy of you.
Henry

What a Time it has Been With(out) You

Another year is ending.

        A year of shutdowns, and reopenings, and mutations

        It was my year with and without you.

        After the dark days of 2020, visiting you was the light at the end of the tunnel

        Without you, but growing close to you, relying, and trusting you more with every returned text and call

        This year has tested both of us. I broke first and popped a question

        You caught me and kept me from falling, and in your wisdom kept me as best friends.

        I feel so many things about having you as my best friend.

        I care about you so much that every time I burst and love bomb you, I have a moment afterward, where I have to pause.

        You mean so much to me that I am filled with excitement at possibly seeing you in May.

        50% excitement at just holding you for a moment in my arms,

        And 50% fear that I am going to be overwhelmed at having you near enough to touch

        that my feelings for you are going to break the dam that they have already overwhelmed and spill by the floodful, over its crest enough to bring enough tears to trigger instant apologies.

You have been here for me this year, even far away

This year will be a special one in memory because of you

And yet…

2022 may be even better if I can control my feelings and leave you feeling as lucky to have me, as I am you

2021 was a year of distant support, and being overwhelmed at how close we have become.

2022, I hope is the year, when we both experience the joy of gratitude that two such amazing people have found each other.

What a time it has been with(out) you

Thank you for being a friend

on this journey, I couldn't have asked for a better companion.

Henry

Pretty Girls

Nineteen years old, hot stuff
      Swinging dick, I was enough
      To catch the eye of every pretty girl,
      Not one of them is now attracted to me.
      Cocky, hot, complacent, fit as a fiddle,
      Now the women I should like, care about that very little.
      The women who make me happy, and I should drool over,
      Are the ones who care about things like *Boba Fett* and *RBG*, and not being my mother
      Finding a woman who I secretly feel,
      Catches the eye of every shallow fool, hoping to steal,
      Her number, her naked, her time with them,
      This is nice, but a woman with whom I am happy to spend,
      A night at the movies, or joking about buying me a lap dance in a club,
      Making real memories, rather than just being imagined for a rub,
      There are a few people who I still want to call,
      Even after two years of awkward lulls,
      Of good gifts and awful, of sexy stories and bad poems never read,

You are someone who is right in my head.

While we may never be naked in the same room, house, or anywhere seen by the other,

You're the one who I know all my standards have recovered,

Even if not you, you have helped me accept I am worthy of love,

A bond like ours is the model I want.

You have shown me what both beauties are,

Inside and outside, from 900 miles afar.

Henry

Good Cheese Love Bomb

In this corporate world,
        Where it seems like everything can come at a price,
        We found each other,
        We marched for what is right,
        Before we even knew how right for each other we were.
        Ours is built on the foundation of what is right.
        Our first steps together
        On this beautiful journey, we have been on together
        Were for what is right.
        I got to hold your hand,
        As we walked through that crowd,
        Of thousands of others there to do right.
        Ours has the blessing of every good and caring person,
        Who has ever loved, fought, and lost a loved one
        For what is right.
        We have such a strong foundation,
        That nothing can knock us down
        Nothing can end us, not forever at least.
        When I write to you,
        Everything good in the world,
        Flows through my heart for you

The words of gentle sweet support for you
Are all my mind holds for you.
Good cheese love bombs
That is how I hold you in my arms,
Or hold your hand,
Or light our way.
Telling you, every day
How wonderful you are
Because of what ours is built on,
Comes like an act of nature.
My appreciation, respect, and fondness for you
Comes on like a storm,
Breaking every man-made obstacle,
And obstruction between me and you.
Our storm
Blows, pours, and breaks
Everything whose foundation
Isn't built on the strong foundation of good
That we took our first steps together
I love telling you how lucky I am,
To become someone that the woman
Who took her first steps with me chose,
On the solid foundation of good,
Would find the words to also praise you,
Because of how much you have broken
All the barriers between us, as we took our first steps

To a better world,
Even just between the two of us
As our storm rages
My everything for you,
Will fall like
Good cheese love bombs
And we will shatter,
The evil we marched against
And build a better world
Free of every evil,
That has no chance,
Of facing us
As we stood on our foundation
And now journey together
As supportive. And worthy
Of each other.

Henry

Without You

On the cold long nights
    I am up, unable to sleep
    Without you

    Even if you were here
    I do fear
    That my sleep
    Would be disturbed
    But not because
    I worry
    But because I want
    To remember every second
    With you

    To have you by my side
    To feel your warmth
    To hear your laugh
    To hold you
    And have you
    To know that I
    Was right where I belong
    That is peace
    That is being.
    Without want.

    To spend our day
    Together

How it ends
I do not know
But the day we spend
Together,
Is a day
I am without need
Other than your grace.

Henry

Safe

Safe,

    From anything.

    What are scars
    On my arms,
    From a bear's attack
    I will not lapse
    In my honor to keep you
     Safe

    What are insults,
    From an angry twit,
    Yelling that,
    I have no right,
    To fight
    To defend your honor
    Keeping her
    Safe

    What is time,
    Spent by your side,
    But a privilege
    Worth all the riches,
    Just for you,
    To feel completely
    Safe

What is another man
But fun for my friend
While I have the knowledge
She will never be forgotten
And as I am allowed
To never stand down,
From standing guard
Over her heart.
Happy she is
Safe

What is pride
But stepping aside
As you are free
Owing nothing to me
But your blessing
For me to hold the feeling
That with me in your life
You will always feel,
Safe.

Henry

Amen

She is coming to see me!
Thank you, Jesus!
Amen.

I get to see her in person
Am I worthy?
Give me strength,
To be my best.
Amen.

I get a chance to be with her
Am I good enough for her?
Give me strength
To be my best.
Amen.

I get to hold her and be in her presence
Will she feel my love for her?
Give me strength
To be my best.
Amen.

Will my one chance change her stance?
Will she see me as someone she wants more of?

Give me strength
To be my best.

Amen.

Will she see, the love inside of me?
Will she smile or will she run?
Give me strength
To be my best.
Amen.

I do not know what will happen
I want so much, but hold close my hopes
Give me strength
To be my best.
Amen.

Henry

It Hasn't even Happened, yet, I Know

There is a day,
In the future,
That I spend with you
I know it will be special
I know I will be fulfilled

It hasn't even happened, yet, I know
It will be one of the best days of my life.
We could sit in silence
It could be completely awkward
Yet having you here with me
Sitting in awkward silence
In my room, my safe space
Fills me with such joy,
That I know heaven on earth is real.

We could do anything
Anywhere
It could rain
Or be blisteringly hot
And still, I know
My future day with you
Will be like living in pure joy

I will and do love you
I have any and every way

You will allow
Best friend, or anything else
I am the luckiest man
To share this future day with you
Even if nothing happens
I will feel like
I had a day worth living
And if you feel the same
I will know
That I have done right
by you

         I look forward   to the   best day of my life   yet to come.

Henry

Communication

I'm sorry.
Did you like that?
How does this feel?
Thank you.

I like that.
That was a good gift.
I don't like you seeing me that way.
Good to know.

What would you like?
Can I hold your hand?
I am sorry I kissed you without asking.
It is OK.

Would you marry me?
No, I won't.
Will you still be my friend?
Yes, of course.

I want to quit smoking.
I wish you would.
When we are eighty?
Yes, then you can rock my world.

Can I send you my poems?
They aren't really my thing.

They are how I process my feelings.
You do you.

When will you visit?
I don't know yet.
Can I have at least one day with you?
Oh yes, you bet.

Henry

Monday Morning without You

What would it be like to wake up next to you?

Would the sun shine brighter?
Or would it dim, to give me few
More precious moments inspired?
To thank every good force in this world
For letting me sleep
Next to the woman I hold
In my dreams, now next to me
Would the birds all chirp
Or would the window be closed
To give us a hint
That our time together without most
Distractions, or conflicts
As you sleep in my arms,
Completely safe, from all, but my lips
How I hope you succumb to my charm.
I want everything about you
To climax, then sleep next to me
I want to be your knight, Viking, and guardian
And to win the role of being with you.

Henry

When Words are all I Have

    When I cannot hold you, or even your hand,
    When I cannot even hold the door for you,
    When I cannot pick you up from work
    When I cannot take you out to dinner
    When I cannot sit in a movie theater with you
    When I cannot walk with you through a bookstore
    When I cannot go yet to a strip club with you
    When I cannot go yet to Disney World with you
    When I cannot go on a walk with you
    When I cannot run through the rain with you,
    When I cannot be filmed by you as I smash fruit
    When I cannot bring you toilet paper
    When I cannot cook you dinner
    When I cannot dance to your records
    When I cannot push your cart into the grocery store
    When I cannot make a fool of myself singing badly in public to you

When I cannot do any of these things, and countless more

When my words are all I have,
When all I can do is send you gifts with the hope,
That when you feel my presence even for the second
As you open them,
I will use my limitations
And yes, maybe go overboard,
But
When my words are all I have,
I will find a way to use them to feel your presence,
And hopefully, capture a moment between us
If only on a page, or screen.
I feel all the feels
And will share all the words.
I miss you.

Henry

Only a Woman, Only You

When a man who never felt comfortable
With his own smile
Can't stop showing it to the world.
That is because of a woman,

When I think of my smile
I think of the years of frowns
I think of you
My smiles abound

Only a woman,
Only you
Could make me laugh at all my sadness
And put a springing step into

I am filled with happiness
I am filled with joy
With you in my life
Life is that which I want more

You, and only you
are the cause of so many smiles,
I could name them all,
But the number of ways to say your name
is kind of small

You,

Make music sweeter
And cold days warmer
You are my best friend

And make me smile every day.

Henry

I Want to Give You

I want to give you what you want
I want to give you what you need
I want to give you what you desire
I want to give you the best time of your life

Every day, you are a part of my life
I have the best day yet
I want to give you the best of me
I want to please your expectations

I want you to feel the way
Only you, make me feel
I want to give you the best time
I want you for life

I will do anything
To be what you want
To do what you need
I feel fulfilled with you

I want to see you smile
And get the high of knowing
I did that to you
I want you to want to smile

I wish I could be the man
Whose job is to take care of you
If there comes a day when you want anything
I want to be the person who gives it to you

You are so much more than a text
Or voice on the other end of a call
You are my heart's guiding star
And with you all is right.

Henry

Strong Enough to let Me

I can hold you, all of you,
Your everything
And just being allowed to be
Strong enough for you
Makes me a man
For you to trust
I want you to feel safe
With or without me
Being your man
Who is strong enough for you
To be what you need me to be
For you to know and feel
That I am strong enough
For all of you
For all your trust
All your fears
All your wants
All your dreams
To be the man
Who is allowed to be strong
for you
Makes my time with you
Worth every second.
I will lift your sorrows
I will humble my pride
I will fight to protect you
So you feel safe inside.

I want to be as strong
As you need
And let me be
A man; how you feel
Is a reflection of me.

Henry

You are Enough

The world could end,
And everything I own could go
With this poem, as it is sent
I want you to know

Even if everything I have
And everything I know
Were to disappear tomorrow
If I still had you, I wouldn't be mad

You are enough
To meet my every need
Living in a tent
With you, I would feel an absence of greed

Eating out of cans
Or apples from trees
If I have you
I have no other needs

You are my star
That lights my nights
Without anything else
My world is still right

I could lose everything
But if you were still with me

I would know without distractions
What it still means to be happy.

Henry

You Got my Back

When the world is against me,
You stand and fight
For what is right
You have my back.

How can anything hope
To take us on together
I have yours,
And you have my back.

Bring them on.
Anything thinks it has a chance
Is fooling itself.
Cause we have each other's backs

I'll take the front
You take my back
Clear them out
Fallen enemies are racked

I got your six
You have mine
Perfect pair, with you
Getting my back, all is fine

Cut 'em down
For trying to fight

Me and you at each other's backs
Attacking us isn't bright.

Henry

Hassle

More than three months till you are here
Every tick of the clock till you are with me
Is a
Hassle

Thirty-five more poems, to fill the void
Of you being far away
Can only be described
As a
Hassle

Every night with you apart
Is another rough night
Just getting through
Is a
Hassle

Less cigarettes
More lotion and showers
Today not being the day
I see you
Is a
Hassle

Tick tick
Goes that annoying clock
Reminding me

That I must wait
But waiting for you
Is what I must do
Even though
It is a
Hassle.

Henry

Afterward, Just Snuggles

I am done, you did me in
I collapsed, you tapped me out
I do not know what you need
I do not know if I have enough
But after you are done with me
Will you stay, at that moment
Together next to each other
Vulnerable, and exhausted
I feel bad, I didn't last
But will you stay with me?
Will you take care of me?
After I have given you everything I had?
Will you still see me as worthy?
After you have conquered me?
Am I enough to stay with afterward?
Will you be cool with me not having words?
And just staring into your eyes,
As my mind and body recover
From what you just did to me
Will you stay?
Will you smile, after filling me
With your endurance?
Will you resist?
Or am I enough?
Even afterward,
Just for cuddles.

Henry

Committed

A year, walking around my backyard
Lost, alone, only able to talk to myself
Finally, they came, and I found myself in the hospital
Eleven months of refusing treatment
What was there to be alive for,
Let alone live
Then the right meds found me
And I was sent back
But what is life, without purpose,
Is being alive all there is?
I strayed, and I wondered.

Then I found myself once again being committed,
Even to a friendship, which fills me with a reason to live life to the fullest.
A friendship, even during lockdown, 900 miles between us
I have been committed against my will, and saved
Your friendship is one I have found myself committed to again
But I would choose you, every day of the year.
You share my life, even from afar
I know love, even of a friend,

I know reason, I know hope
I know why I am alive
I know what fills my life
You and I found each other,
We marched, we ate, we talked,
And I found inside of myself love,
Love for life and love for living my life,
I am grateful for my previous commitment
For letting me live
I am grateful for my current commitment,
Because I now have an anchor as to why,
Why commitment is a good thing
And why my life is a gift and a special thing to experience.

Henry

It Beats Again

        Your music fills me with emotion
        You make my heart beat again
        A stolen kiss, even without a future white dress
        You make my heart beat again

        A cardboard cutout, under your bed
        You make my heart beat again
        A day at the ballpark, three foul balls none of them yours
        You make my heart beat again

        You drove, caught Covid, went out to Olive Garden
        You make my heart beat again
        I brought paper for your ass
        You make my heart beat again

        I got you a ring that says reserved, I forced the point
        You make my heart beat again
        I ruined your Christmas, you had to say, "No."
        You make my heart beat again

        You stayed my friend, we watched *End Game* till the end

You make my heart beat again
You got annoyed when I called too much, I was off the phone in a rush
You make my heart beat again

You moved away, I had to stay
You make my heart beat again
You shared your wishlist, I bought you a record from it
You make my heart beat again.

You owe me nothing, but still, give me what's overwhelming
You make my heart beat again
You are a good person; I am grateful that you listen
You make my heart beat again.

Henry

Door to Door

      Warehouse to door, in a day
      Such an easy and convenient way
      To show you I care, and for me to say
      Even with 900 miles between us, no obstacle will stay

      Between me and you, and how I feel
      With you in my life, life seems more real
      A same coast apart, yet I can deal
      With giving you my heart, and with hopes of yours to steal

      I may not be able to hold or see
      But because of your laptop, I can be
      With you in my room, your smile will tease
      A smile out of me, for a shared moment of distant separate glee

      Door to door, I want you to come
      To visit and stay, for more than fun
      I want to smell you, to feel you, for this distance to be done
      To me, even as a friend, you are the one.

      Who is to say, what lies ahead?
      Is it a bookstore, or a shared bed?

Is it a day out, with signs to be read?
Or is it just accepting my heart I have led

Into fool's territory, into deception and lies

Now closed, do I need to open my eyes?
That you have been clear, and my romance needs to die

Or when we are together, will we both be surprised?

Henry

Florida, Lucky Florida

Made up, looking hot
Make-up on, breaking my neck
So, smoking hot, looking good
What I wouldn't give that good girl.

How does such an unworthy state,
House the girl of my dreams?
What I wouldn't do to be with her
Just to show her what she deserves.

I felt my heart jump,
I felt my lips dry
If she was with me
I'd be so happy I could die

She looked like every fantasy I've had
Of beautiful women out of my league
I am afraid I blow it when she's here
Tender kisses are just sweet dreams

Florida, you lucky bastards
How dare you share in her hotness
If I could, I would sever you into the ocean
And have her all to myself

Florida, my jealousy of you
Brings me down to your level

Why do you get the girl of my dreams?
And I get shafted?

Florida, you have what I want
I declare out of spite
A fight for her, the most attractive
You stand no chance in this duel for satisfaction

Fuck you Florida, she should be mine.
You have done nothing to deserve her.
If you think this is over, to yourself you're lying
This will not end well for you Florida

Henry

I Want to Show You, My Everything

I want to send you the world,
I want to show you, my everything
I want to bare my soul
I want to strip off the mystique
I want to show you, my everything

I want to take off all that separates us
I want to wear nothing that hides
My unclad and raw feelings for you
I want to show you, my everything

I want to expose all that I have
And give you what I have for you
I want to give you my everything
I want to share all of me with all of you

I want to show you my naked heart
I want you to see how hard it has been to be apart
I want to grasp all my girth down below
And to you, I want to show
I want to show you, my everything

I want you to see, Mr. Happy
When I show you all that I have hidden from you

I want to click a pic, of my hidden treasure
That is most moved by you

I want to send it to you and catch your eye
What it means for me to be a guy
And be in love with you
I want to show you, my everything.

Henry

The Unthinkable, Love

      A year, wandering lost,
      In my parent's backyard,
      Only able to speak to me,
      Jail, Western State, jail, NVMHI
      Eleven months of treatment back and forth
      Just to sleep through the night,
      And jolt a nurse with shock,
      When I shared, "I think I'm starting to feel better."

      The unthinkable thought has found me.
      In my love for you, it swirls around my thoughts,
      Do I love you enough to never allow the possibility?
      Of ever letting you see me like this, if it happens again?

      Or do I need you so deeply
      That I would allow myself to be selfish

      Do I need you so badly?
      Is my love so deep for you?
      That I would allow
      The woman I love,
      A chance to have her heartbroken
      If my mind breaks again?

Is a selfless life my only choice?
Is sparing you, myself,
The only way I can do right by you?

I cannot live another day,
Without allowing myself selfish thoughts
Of allowing myself the chance to break your heart
For mine to feel whole.

I am going to propose again,
Not marriage, but
A willingness to allow me to be selfish.

The National Alliance on Mentally Illness
NAMI
Maybe a place you have to turn to one day,

Will you allow me to be selfish?
In my needs, wants, and thoughts?

Would you join NAMI for me?
https://www.nami.org/home?

Henry

Vulnerable

Swords, axes and spears,
All hundreds of years away
From common damage,
Guns are dangerous
But to me these fears
Are distant and manageable
The words I share,
And the fear,
Of you saying four words to me
Makes every armor and precaution
Helpless, futile and useless
No bullet will ever get as close
To killing my heart
No spear will ever harm me
As much as the pain and irreparable damage
Of four words coming from you,
My dream, my fantasy, my biggest hope, my only prize
Would destroy every cell in my body,
Four words from you, would kill my spirit
And leave my soul without a desire to go on
Four words from you
Are more dangerous than every weapon ever made
The four words which I must never allow

>   To be felt enough for you to say,
>   The four words which I have no defense
> against
>   The four words:
>   "I don't love you."
>   If I ever earn, will be my end.
>
>   Henry

Fun and Despair

Single, absolute freedom
Freedom to
Fuck whoever
Buy whatever
Do whatever

But single means I don't have you.

All my fun, all my irresponsible
Extended childhood

Fills me with despair
That I don't have you

A pound of flesh
Or a gnawed-off limb
Is where my single life
Takes my mind.

Trapped in empty meaninglessness without you

I would choose to limit all my reckless
Irresponsible hedonism
Of my life being single

If it meant I could call you mine,

And my life was to
Respectfully, and equally
And happily, be yours.

Henry

Freebie Giveaways

A record, a bracelet, s shield with a star
A cheap infinity gauntlet, whose fingers don't move
Gifts of love, and affection for my friend.

But my biggest gift is not free,
For me, giving it is so costly to you
Because when I give it to you,
If you do not pay, with the same
Then it is a gift that is unwelcome and unwanted

I give you all gifts freely,
Just knowing I got you something
Special or funny, or heartfelt
Pays emotional rewards back to me

But one gift, I have for you
With your name on it
With you in mind when I give it to you
Requires you to accept it,
And give to me your equal

My heart is yours
I want to give it to you
But this is a gift that is not fun to refuse
And not easy to match

My heart is packaged,
With your name on it
I hold it back,
Because to require the same
If not given with joy and love
Means I have damaged both
And that is a bad gift to give.

Henry

Keep it Up

Keep it up, you are free
I am far away, and unable
To do somethings, for you

Keep it up, I will not be deterred
Florida men have you now
But I will only need one day
To show you true love

Keep it up, I will wait for you
Fleeting fun is not strong enough
To hold you, with the gentlest tough
In love more than any words can capture

Keep it up, my time is coming
My one day, to brush all the sleep
Off your and my dreaming eyes
And make real my love for you

Keep it up, I will still love you
I will be all the man you need
For a day, you will know your womanhood
It is hell to wait, but you will find heaven
When you are with me, even for at least a day

Keep it you, you are only young once
But my love is of the ages
Legendary love is what awaits you here.

Keep it up, you are not mine
Yet.

Henry

Black Kool-Aid

I drank you in, your black Kool-Aid
I bought in, I emptied my glass
I drank every last drop
I love your black Kool-Aid
All I want to drink for the rest of my life
Is your black Kool-Aid

It is sweeter and more fulfilling
Then any other drink I have, or will ever have
I want to sip from your pitcher
I want to stir your glass
I want to taste it, every night
On my tongue
I want to lick your black Kool-Aid
From the deepest crevices of your cups

Yours is incomparable
Because it blows all the others away
Will you give me just one more sip?
Of your black Kool-Aid,

Every day without it,
Is a century in the driest desert?
My lips need your black Kool-Aid
My body is addicted, hopelessly
To your magical concoction

You are my black Kool-Aid
And I have never been happier
To have you
as the only
and best
Choice.

Henry

To Leave my Tree

Loneliness is universal
Everyone feels it,
Or are susceptible to it
Even the crazy

At the three-month mark, of my last crisis
Of walking around my parents' backyard
Pausing only for periods
When I would sit and smoke
On a one-foot-high wall of bricks,
My dad had taken from his garden,
I started to commune with my tree.

I was so lonely, and the tree was so strong
And tall, and marvelous.
I stared at the tree and tried to will it awake
I was deep in grad school for an MS in biology
I knew better but wanted a friend
I focused my mind
Past the point, anyone in crisis should be able

For the next three months
I spoke, hugged, and willed my tree
Trying to make it wake up
I wanted it to come alive and walk with me

I wanted an Ent friend
And I was just lonely and crazy enough,
To try to make it happen for real

At the six-month mark of my crisis
I gave up
But I made a pact with my tree
The one that sits out my back window
If I ever was unworthy,
Or became an agent of harm
That my tree
Had full authority to be my judge
For over thirty years it has sat outside my window
Eight since my oath.
I have not been judged as unworthy by my tree
It has yet to fall and take me out.

But there is a realization
Love is more powerful than judgement
My tree has until you accept me as yours
Into your heart
Then you will become my judge
And with our hearts rooted deep into each other's
Like my tree's roots deep in the earth
I will no longer fear loneliness ever again.

My tree watches over me
Can come to an end
When you are ready to put down roots with me

My tree stood strong for me for almost my whole life

I am ready to stand strong for you.

Will you give me a reason?
To leave my tree.

Henry

That Terrifying Feeling

Cigarettes are a powerful addiction
They give life a purpose when all else is meaningless

Love is a powerful force
It gives a meaningless life reason

I am addicted
I am in love

And now I find myself with
That terrifying feeling

Is my addiction, that is killing me,
More powerful than my love for you?

I want you so bad, I want to keep you
I want a war, between my addiction and my love

But there is
That terrifying feeling

That I am too far gone
That I have lost my way

Can someone who has ventured

Into such depths of meaninglessness

Can I come back and break it off,
With the one thing that kept me going?

A test of my faith
Is my love more powerful than my addiction?

To fail is to discover truth in
That terrifying feeling

To succeed, guarantees me nothing
But a chance to show you the strength

Behind my words, every time I say
"I am in love with you."

Henry

Will my Love for you Keep it Full?

My heart is full, with love for you
A box sits full on my shelf,
Will my love for you keep it full?

Twenty times ten is the number that fills
200 inside, chances to show
How full my heart is for you.

In a day, week, month, or year,
Will 200 still stand unburnt,
Will my love beat my addiction?

200 soldiers, tempting me into war
Every minute of every day
Will my love for you keep it full?

I do not know if this war will be won
But I have a reason to fight
Keeping the 200 soldiers unlit, unburnt

Each breath I take
With the 200 not inhaled
Is a test of my love for you

Six weeks is when the first sign
Of success will appear

Will my love for you keep it full?

When I kiss you, I do not want
The stench of my death
To be on my lips

Will my love for you keep it full?

Henry

25-4

If I get the chance to kiss you when you visit,

I want to look into your eyes,
And tell you, "I'm in love with you."
I want to lean in and feel
Your sweet soft lips touch mine
I want to give you a moment
Where you know
That I truly love you
I want you to know that
My love for you is real,
And more powerful
Then even my addiction

Twenty-five cigarettes a day on a good day

Four cigarettes today.

I am proud of this accomplishment

But each of the four
Was like a railroad spike
To my heart

That I was risking
And hurting
A chance of
That moment

With you.
If love is real,
Then there is more than
My desire to have you
To give you
My everything
For just a day

If love is real
Then it isn't just
A biological attraction
It is something more

My love feels so deep
But with each of the four
I asked if it was just a delusion
Rooted somewhere
Less deep than my addiction

25-4
Sounds like a good score

But I want a blowout
For me against my addiction
And in your heart,
If I ever get to kiss you.

Henry

So Hard

A night of fun for you
Makes living 900 miles away
So hard.

Even without the slight jealousy
Not being able, to be an option
Is so hard.

Another coffin nail
Up to five
So hard

No texts on date night
That would be controlling
So hard

Maybe she won't check her email
So, I don't look so pathetic, until tomorrow
So hard

Self-judgement finds me
Low nicotine exacerbates
So hard

Am I becoming a stalker?
Am I just obsessed?

So hard

Am I just a creep?
And has my addiction blinded me
So hard

Do I owe a thousand apologies?
Or is my silence way overdue?
So hard

I wish I could sleep for a month
Just let the nicotine drain from me.
So hard.

Henry

Do I know? or, do I just Hope?

Do I know for the day that you are here
That you are going to rock my world?
Or do I just hope?

Do I know that I am going to have trouble
Meeting you at the airport?
Because just standing in front of you
Is going to be awkward?
Or do I just hope?

Do I know that there will be a sloppy kiss?
And you will be so overcome,
That you tackle me to the ground?
As we are overcome and make out
At the airport?
Or do I just hope?

Do I know we will blow off all other activities,
That require clothes, or leaving my room?
Or do I just hope?

Do I know that you will break the mold,
Of every other woman, I have ever been with?

Or do I just hope?

Do I know my room is going,
To have your scent, for at least a week?
Or do I just hope?

Henry

I Have no Idea

I have no idea if you are in love with me
I have no idea if you ever will be
I have no idea if you even read
Any of my poetry

I have no idea if I am annoying
Or something far worse than boring

I have no idea if you are just a friend
An infatuation that needs to end

I have no idea if I have made you regret
Ever allowing me to fret
About a visit that you might let
My dream come true, or end even a friendship

I have no idea how you feel
To be fair, you have set boundaries

I have no idea if I am pushing you
Towards something you don't want
I have no idea of your patience with me
Is just a front

I have no idea if I have only one more chance

Or if the friendship or more till our end
will last

I have no idea if I have fooled myself
Into startling you to being something else
Then you are comfortable
Then you want to be,
If I have, I am prepared for you to leave
As disappointed in my disrespect
For putting you through such heck

I have no idea if I have scared you
Even if there are times I do
And there I times I see my woo's
As well received, As helping see my best
But if I need to stop, now is when to tell
me
To give it a rest.

Henry

Cancer

Fear is a gift, that is what has been said.
I feared for years, of my early death.
Then everything collapsed, and
Just by breathing, I felt rich
Deep depression, psychosis, and anxiety
Living was a bitch.
Cancer is not something I fear any more
I probably should, but to me, it is a bore
I have no fear because I have faced what to me felt worse
But then the thought of you, standing next to my hearse
That doesn't scare me, but it fills me with guilt
For me to ask you to be with me while risking bringing on hell
That is cruel, is mean, and an objectionable thing to do,
But after smoking my third smoke of the day, the impossibility of giving this up turns me to,
The observation, that step by step, I hope to break through
To quit smoking so I can honor you
Maybe medicine will leap forward, maybe I will be safe,
But giving up smoking shakes me more than getting my own place.

If there is a way, to pit my love against my addiction

Then I have a strong anchor, as my motivation.

Cancer means so much to you because you care about people, you do,

Cancer to me means just an odious smell, and being accused of being rude.

I am not excited, but if I am going to quit,

My motivation will be more than just friendship.

Friends die, so do pets

But happily ever after for you, is why I am trying to quit.

Stay silent, do not respond, that is the way this works,

But this gesture, which benefits me the most, is mostly for how to you, I look.

Henry

Anything You Want

    Anything you want,

    That is what you can do.
    It is not even my place for me to forgive you.

    Be brave, be bold, be free and true
    That is what I want from me to you.

    I need you to push the limits of what you can do,
        For me to know that you are comfortable you being you.
        Trust and strength are necessities for you to push through
        For me to know I am never controlling you

    If you want to yell or do anything for you,
        Then I need to grow to be a man, strong and worthy for you to choose
        I want to build you up and support your every new
        Day living your life completely true

        I want to build trust where your limits are not used
        I want you to fly in every formation or free, the day we met, never being rued

        I will learn to say nothing if that is what is best for you
        To feel my feelings and grow to accept that being selfish is worse than rude

        A moment of rejection is not mine to refuse
        If you ever need any support or distance, I will give it to you
        I see now how much growth I have to do
        But growing by your side I am far from refuse

        I have my own dreams, and only a part of my life is yours too
        But the time we spend together is the best way I could hope to use
        My responsible self and responsibilities to you.
        That is my vision of a shared life, an adventure anew.

        Henry

One Shelf

When I think about our time knowing each other

So much of it has been from afar
Only a few outings
Shows you have seen, but I haven't watched

Our time together in each other's presence
Has been so limited
Like one shelf of memories
Then a tall empty bookcase waiting for more

I want to fill my bookshelf
With memories of you
I want to write each chapter
Fill each book, with our stories

Yes, over the past two years
It has felt like the world has shut down
But my all-but-empty bookcase of
Time with you is ready to be filled

What would you do,
if I lived there, Or you here
Would it involve a couch or bed?
Of would we make the world our oyster?

I love the few books of memories
That we have made together
But a long life, with you as part of it
Inspires my sense of adventure.

Henry

I'll Know

Within five seconds of seeing you
I'll know
Whether you are just being polite
Or if there is a seed to grow.

When you say hello,
From the tone of your voice
I will sense the anxiety of a future partner
Or a friend and that is all

When I hug you
I'll know
If we are bonded in love
Or if you want nothing more

When we laugh
I'll know
The laugh of two in love
Or just the comfort of the familiar

When we talk
I'll know
If everything I feel
Is reciprocated

I'll know
You know

If when our eyes meet
They find in each other home

Henry

One Side of the Equation

$450,000 is the budget
The price of a townhouse
Down payment of $90,000
That's 20%
Then $2,000 a month for thirty years

I have $27,000 saved
I make $51,423 a year gross
I save $2,100 a month in net
If the stock market makes better than average gains of %20 a year
In May of 2023, I could have
Around $72,000 saved

If I got the biggest possible raise in September 2022, I have had estimated to me
I would be able to have saved $76,000 by May of 2023
That would be 16% of a down payment for a $450,000 townhouse
If I went 10% down, I would have a cushion of $31,000 as an emergency reserve

All of this to say, I am serious about you.
All of this is to say I am a man to be taken seriously by you.
All of this to say, please take me seriously

All of this to say, I want the job of taking care of you.

Henry

Breaking my Back, to Break Yours

Sixty poems, at an accelerating rate
All so that 'us' can be our fate
Make me want you more
If that is even possible
I'm breaking my back,
To have a chance to break yours.

I want you bad, in my arms,
And in my bed
Anything you want,
To get my hunger for you fed.

I want you so bad,
If tonight was an option
I'd run night a thousand miles,
To fill your oven.

You are hot, you're my fantasy
You bring me to
A place where my body turns to steam

Anything that does it for you,
Will do it for me
I am ready to please you
To get me pleased too.

How long, how hard?
I hope you wonder too.
But baby I'm yours
If you let me make love to you.

Henry

My Sacred Scottish Honor

I am spoke and support you
My black queen,
But there is something
Up my kilt,
That is begging to be seen.

You are who I want and need
Not just any woman, but mine, to be
I have to tell you, to make things fair
That this is more to me than
Breaking your back, while I pull your hair

I want you to be mine,
I never want to lose you
I will be a good man to you
But being together
I need you to find

In yourself, a strong resolve
I stand your ground
When it is time to resolve
This silence between us
I will wait for now

But when we are together,
If I am to hold you tight
Your love for me,

Must be stronger than one fight,

I will honor, obey
Treat you right
But be prepared
To tell me at the end of the night

If what we are,
If what I hold
Is more than emails
Hoping for you to behold

Examine yourself,
Bring your terms
If I am to be yours
You, I am ready to earn

Light fun fucking
Or merely joking by text
Is all well and good
But I ask you not to ignore the rest

In my Scottish honor
My heart is yours
Now you must ponder
If mine you wish to hold.

Henry

It Hurts to Write This

It hurts to write this, now that I fear
Even doing so is against your wishes.

I would give you all of myself
If you were just to desire me.

I want more of you, than you of me
But my heart still beats for you

I want to hold you, as my own
I want you to feel free in my arms

In this big world of awful things
I want you to be my home

I want you to feel at home with me
And to know I will never abandon you

You are more than I will ever know
But even as a friend, you fulfill most of me

I want you to shatter, in such a specific
way

Just let me though, and nothing else

But for us to be is not to be
And knowing that makes writing

My love for you hurt so deeply.

Henry

You are my Whole Mood

When you smile, I light up inside
When you fear, I fill with rage
When you laugh, my life has meaning
When you cry, my whole purpose is to comfort you

When you feel, I feel about you
I want to change the world
Just so you can feel often
How I feel about you always

You are the one, who I want
To hold and make my love known too
I want to take all your pain
And leave you only with strength

I want your softness
I want to be soft with you
I want you to lift me up
Simply by letting me do the same for you

You own my heart
And I gave it to you freely
Every day with you
Is my heart's best day yet

Thank you for being my one

Thank you for letting me feel
Thank you for giving me aim
Thank you for allowing
To feel alive with you.

Henry Johnson

I Would Never, unless it Fulfilled You

I would never be harsh or unkind,
Unless in a moment of passion
It fulfills your desire

I would never be rude or thoughtless
Lazy, weak, apathetic, or disloyal
Unless that was what you wished for me
In a moment that lead me to satisfy you

I would never fail to support you
I will catch you if you fall,
Give you my everything
If that is what you need from me

I would never put you second
Or spare a single thought for duties to another above you
Unless that is what made you love me more

I would never forgive any unkindness to you
Any enemy of yours is my enemy
Unless you desired peace
And following your lead, I will forgive
If that fills you with comfort

I would never ask anything of you,
That didn't make you happy to give.
Being your rock, pillow, or pillar which keeps your sky from falling
Is what I am prepared to give
If it satisfies you.

Henry

Claimed by Another

There you were sitting five feet away,
Then she claimed me,
And at that moment, I could feel
The soon-to-be 900 miles between us get in the way

She was special, wonderful, kind, and true
But in the end, she wasn't you
You were the one I wanted
She was the one who gave me a chance

All the time together with her
I never had a single doubt
That everything happens for a reason
And even as friends, you would not be forgotten

You may have been my intention
And she may have stolen me away
But I grew into the man
That I could be what everyone respected

She is now a friend,
As are you
But how I hope while she and my road has ended

Yours and mine is just about to begin

I have no expectations
I have no demands
Even the most awkward day ever with you
Would be one I treasure forever

So know I never put you second
And now that you have a chance to be my number one
I prepare myself for a chance
To enter heaven.

Henry

Date Me, My Friend

Date me,
Please, ask me to be yours
I want you to ask me
I have asked and will not ask again
I want you, to let me
To be the one who fulfills you
To be the one who loves you first
To be the one whose job is to protect you
To take care of you, to grow to be what you want
Just open the door,
I will not stay out here
And while I am not in the cold,
In your heart, as yours,
Would be like walking inside
Out of the warm spring rain
of your friendship.
If that door is opened,
And I am asked inside,
I will not forget the sweet raindrops,
And beautiful spring flowers that bloomed
And now gently hold the warm drops of rain on their petals,
While waiting outside, in the garden
Of your friendship.
Inside your heart,
is where I want to make a home.

While here, in the warm rain,
Fairies may visit, and tell me
Tales of how lucky I am,
In the garden of your friendship.
This beautiful place where I find myself now,
Will never be forgotten,
Or left behind,
If I am ever invited
Inside your heart.

Henry

In Limerence, or Love?

Does something magic have to exist,
Something more than atoms, and energy,
For love to be more than a fairytale?

Does there need to be an absolute
A physical tangible soul
For love to be more than can be quantified?

If I were to kiss your breast,
Would there have to be a spark,
Or would you have to be proven to
That my lips on your breast were more
Then what do anatomy textbooks define?

Sixty-eighth poem
Is that all the proof I need
To cry, "Limerence! Limerence!"
And accept that I am injuring my rational mind?

Did you ask me to stop?
Because my words were rough,
Unwanted, and unacceptable?
Did I get my answer?
Do I have my proof?

Or are my words too true
For you?
Is there magic in poetry,
Which is powerful enough,
To move,
To stir,
To challenge the comfort between us?

Is there magic in my love for you?
Or am I just in,
Limerence?

Henry

Is my Love for you, Corrupting?

Unrequited, yes.
Unreciprocated, yes
Deep and foundational, yes
But corrupting, I do not know.

Does my love for you, spoil,
Because you do not feel the same way?

Am I damaging myself by feeling completely fulfilled,
But wanting you more every day?

Am I lying to myself to keep this sweet delusion of hope,
Growing deeper into the soil which is not my own?

Does love have to be reciprocated,
For it to be more than limerence and obsession?

I have shared my feeling,
You have shared yours.

Because they are not the same
Do I bear the responsibility,

To win your heart,
Or to respect you more?

Am I greedy, twisted, and wrong,
To want you so badly as more,
Than a friend?

There is hope, that your dam will break
When we see each other and hug
But hold you in my heart,
And adjusting my gaze, back to only a friend,
Feels like I am failing out of and failing myself.

Henry

Say it with Love

Call me friend,
Call me boyfriend,
Call me nerd,
Call me kind,
Call me funny,
Call me wicked,
Call me wonderful,
Call me generous,
Call me not for you,
Call me a better match for someone else,
Call me yours,
Call me like-minded,
Call me the one,
Call me late,
Call me early,
Call me Tuesday,
Call me Saturday,
Call me after church,
Call me after movie group
Call me after book group,
Call me after your show,
Call me after work,
Call me to ask for something,
Call me to brag,
Call me to share,
Call me to complain,
Call me special,

Call me too much,
Call me not enough,

Whatever, or whenever
You call me,
Say it with love.

Henry

In Love, In Friendship

My love for you,
May not be the same
As your love for me,

You are my heart's desire
And for you
I am your best friend.

You do love me,
You have made this clear,
But my love is for more
Mine is based on romance
And attraction for you
That yours doesn't seem to be.

Some will take this
As tragic
As a sad end
To this tale,
My heart may need to heal
A bit
But I still have you
As an ally
And in every way
That we love equally
I do not
And should not

Have the power
To change another's heart

But mine is yours
And even though not reciprocated

In love, In friendship,
I still feel grateful
To call myself yours

Henry

I would Break for You

Even a taste of you,
With nothing more,
Would break me.

To see your body,
And never touch,
Would be so much to handle.

If you gave me a chance,
I would want more.
If you just opened the door,
To have a moment with you
And then let you go
Would break me.

But what is the value?
What is the price?
For the greatest moment of my life.
That moment
Would define happiness
It would transcend time
And would live in my mind
For the rest of my life.

To see you,
Bare and beautiful,
Would shatter all ceilings

And blow my mind.
I would love it.

Just a moment with you,
With nothing more
Would break me,
But for that moment,
I would break for you.

Henry

The Chase

From afar you have stood your ground,
I have done my best to stick around.
You have been nothing but clear
All I have is gotten to know you, I fear.
No sign, no words, no change in your view of me
My hope begets disrespect in my refusal to believe.
Will I take in your words spoken true,
Or will I be overcome by my desire for you?
Am I wrong to hope there is something hidden?
Or is that foolishness which I was long ago best ridden?
I have chased you, but you have not run.
Now so close to all it has been is fun
You are no trophy, it looks like you will not be mine,
This was true on this journey's first step, so long it took me to find.
I want to scream a thousand things
Not at you but my foolish journey definitely brings,
Apologies for all the time I have taken
And for every emotional confession
From me to you, with no us to show

Now it is best for me to let it go.
Even now I ask myself,
Does letting you go complete the rest?
Has my chase to make you mine
All been a pursuit where I needed to find
That some are not meant to have and to hold,
But to enjoy as a friend that's all, as we grow old,
Nothing has been sacrificed that won't come with growth
But here a moment of sadness resides in my final hope.
I let no one down, no one was hurt
No bridges between us have been burnt.
But this case has been more like a pursuit of my own tail,
Not every pursuit escapes a fail.
Two months till I see you, time to repair
My expectations returning to fair
This chase is not over, though you have not budged,
But one thing is clear, with you nothing can be rushed.
See you soon, likely as a friend,
The day we meet in person will possibly be your courtship's end.

Henry

How Did we Win this Lottery?

With all the odds that I would find you
We both struck it big and found each other.
A minute chance to match then meet
And now, every day, I am the richest man in the world.
And you are a wealthy woman.
A pair of luck billionaires
Just to have what we have
The odds seem bigger every day
As I fall deeper and deeper in love with you
Being with you would be like a second jackpot
Those impossible odds mean something higher has plans for us
Do I start a search for the abstract, the unscientific?
Does a man with my riches dare pray for more?
Is greed that force which will bring us together?
What else could make such a man, rich with luck, test all he has won?
For you I would sin, but can a sin be called selfless?
If I live the life I hope to live

        Having, holding, protecting, and providing
        Would turning to something that might have a greater cost
        Be wise if we could be meant for more?
        A pinch of selfish greed after all we have won by finding each other
        Just for a tiny nudge into each other's arms
        You are that which I desire
        And I know what I would do
        But greed, whose terrifying kinship
        Fulfills my final desire and finishes the final steps of our lucky journey
        Is now pulling me towards mounting you
        Not as just a fuck, but as all my life's devotion.
        Will greed turn our lottery ticket into
        The birth of a relationship?

        Henry

The End of the Beginning

This is poem number seventy-five
I have written these poems as
A way of processing falling and being
In love with my best friend.
No rhyming
No clever structure
Just a thought
That if or when I see you
And give you this book of my poems
It will be after a long journey as friends
Friends with a one-sided romance.
I do not know if this is a happy ending
I do not know if this book
Will ever be read by anyone other than me
But this book has been a journey for me
   There are likely times I will sound unbalanced and possibly
   Insane
   But I have kept the first seventy-five poems I have written to you
   I thought the best thing I always offered you was my
   True self
Maybe you will read this,
Maybe someone else will
Maybe I have an ounce of talent that
My love and friendship with and for you

world. Has motivated a new work of art into this

If so, I hope it is found at least worthy to exist by someone

I am proud of the journey I have taken
I am proud of the work that I have finished
I hope that there is romantic love with you
In our future
But even if there is not
If even one of these poems speaks or moves

Someone
Then our love even in writing found its wings.

I love you, as a friend, if that is all you will allow.

But what a friend, to take a writer,
And sing in his heart, until
A work of art is born.
Thank you

Forever yours,
Henry

www.ingramcontent.com/pod-product-compliance
Lightning Source LLC
LaVergne TN
LVHW041638060526
838200LV00040B/1616

9 781800 167865